Kindness

Society Today

Mentoring

Unexpected Surprises

Advice and Perspectives

SOMETHING HAPPENED TODAY

A Collection of the Unexpected

Paul E. Kotz

outskirts
press

To all who like a good story.

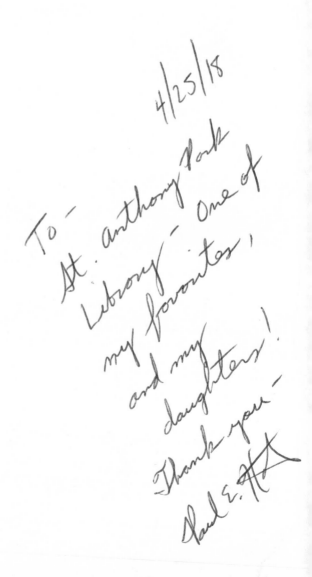

Acknowledgment

Thanks to Sharon Sundre and Linka Holey, who encouraged me to write and finish a book.

To my daughters - Kali and Rebecca, and stepson, Andy. Very proud of you and your own families.

To my friends, family and those who cajoled and inspired me to go into different directions, persuaded me to not settle for the first thing I wrote, and who challenged me to attempt to surpass previous expectations.

To my wife and lifelong companion, Jan - who brings me joy each day, and invites me to be a better man.

Thanks to my publishing consultant Kirsten Ringer, and my author representative, Dana Nelson, for your guidance, professionalism and patience. Joan Rogers - I appreciate your editing advice.

And, thank you to the people who helped mold and shape me to look for the good in life.

You know who you are. If not, I will remind you.

Cover – Photo of Como Park under the Lexington Bridge.
St. Paul, Minnesota
Late Summer, 2017

Table of Contents

Growing Up

Something Happened Today
A Collection of Unexpected Surprises

"Get outside every day. Miracles are waiting everywhere."
Regina Brett

"I expect to pass through this world but once; any good thing
therefore that I can do, or any kindness that I can show to any
fellow creature, let me do it now; let me not defer or neglect it,
for I shall not pass this way again."
Stephen Grellet

Introduction

I attempted to write this book on January 1, 2001, because I wanted to leave something inspiring for my daughters to read when they were older. It is now, 2018, and I can say that this book is a product of many events, gifts and fortuitous unexpected occurrences, which I share with you. I can't say that I am the most fascinating writer ever born, but I have had plenty of experiences that I hope people can either laugh at, possibly learn from, or a combination of both.

Sometimes what compels us to do one thing or another is still unclear to me, but every day I come to some new realization, or some new insight as to how I have acted in different circumstances. And mysteries and nuances of life somehow become clearer.

I think that a person is a collection of his or her own experiences. Much has to do with heredity, I'm sure. I can still see some of my father in me, and plenty of my mother, especially in those quiet moments, when I have time to look back on why I was put on the earth, to begin with.

At the time I started this book, the power went out in our neighborhood, and I thought I lost my set of stories. But, what kind of ego do I have thinking that what I write will or would have any impact on another person? The nerve of some people.

Anyway, before you proceed, I must say that one of the greatest gifts everyone is given is the ability to communicate, and I continue to work on this daily.

So, you mind as well throw this book aside, and start your own book. (I'm just kidding). I want you to stay with me for a while before you throw this hit or miss creation aside.

Also, I start out each day, primarily as a teacher for most of my life saying......

"Help Me to Be a Better Man"

Recently, one of my students said, "How do you remain flexible with us, when we can be so difficult?" It made me reflect on something I say to myself almost every day.

When I wake up, I ask, "God, help me to be a better man."

My wife has also prayed for me, "PLEASE help him be a better man."

Before I walk into the door of every classroom I teach, I say, "Please help me be a good teacher today. Please help me bring kindness, clarity, laughter and joy to people. Please help me heal and never hurt…." This prayer and mantra doesn't always work, and I often, just fail, but it does put me in a better frame of mind to approach the complexities of the day.

This book is about hope. It is about everyday life. It is also about what I observe, react to, and reflect on. There is even some advice, so you can avoid making some of the same mistakes I have made.

I hope this helps you to see that there is much good in the world. We just have to look around us, and that we have the power to make positive impactful changes.

Alison McGhee said, "Every moment of every day you can bring people down or you can lift them up — you, one small person — by the energy you project. We choose what we want our lives to mean, and what we want to leave behind. We have the power to write our own stories. Remember that." It is in this spirit, that these stories are shared.

Help Me to Know Clearly

Another prayer, which I often recite to myself to face life's situations is - "Help me to know clearly the work which I am called to do in my life. And give me the strength to answer your call with courage, love, and lasting dedication to your will. Amen."

The Christian Brothers taught me this when I went to Cretin High School in the late 70's and early 80's. I must say that I had no clue as to what I was saying back then, but have found that today it really guides many decisions I make.

A Close Call That Changed My Perspective

In August of 2003, I had a very close call, where I had a pinhole leak in my appendix that had slowly been poisoning my body for months. Thankfully, my wife Jan took me to the hospital in time, and doctors and nurses helped me recover from serious peritonitis, that would have ended my life. At the time, I had very little hope, when I heard the news of my possible fate. But, doctors performed an emergency appendectomy, and after a day or so, I would get up after surgery with all of the contraptions attached to me, keep my body moving, and banter with the nurses to keep my spirits high, where they would often laugh with me, too. They told me I should stay in bed, but stubbornly, I felt I still had a life to live.

There is no doubt that this experience changed my outlook. After six months, I felt fully recovered, but because of this event, I vowed I would live life to the fullest, and look for the good, no matter the situation. The time we have is so precious.

I had a recent student disclose that they had very little hope for the future, battling depression, bills, work/life balance and relationship issues, not to mention the barrage of negative news. They said, "What is the point?"

Although not a counselor, I thought back to how I felt, when it seemed that hope was lost and when I was scared of what my own future entailed. I am not sure if my encouragement truly helped this individual, but I gave them a few anecdotes where I turned many previous failures into some success, found love where there was some hate, and let them know that they have a life - where their heart is beating, they are breathing, and able to laugh - so there has to be hope, even when it only seems like a glimmering light.

Cicero is credited as saying, "Where there is life, there is hope."

We All Can do Exceptional Things

There are people who think America is on the downslide. Others think we have lost empathy for one another, and some say that people just do not care about their own neighbors, or society.

I would like to offer another viewpoint.

Each day, I see countless examples of people who make America exceptional.

Just recently, I saw someone take the time to send a card around for signatures for an individual who lost their mom. On my way to work, I saw someone stumble on University Avenue and a man with a "Will Work for Food" sign, help her up from the ground, and then resume asking for change. Later that evening, I saw a couple holding hands, and enjoying the time they had together. You could tell that they really cared for one another. The guy had flowers behind his back, and gave them to his love, at the opportune time. And she smiled with a joyful exuberance.

I saw a professor talk about "creating your own happiness." Events can bring us joy and sorrow, but how we react can make a difference in our attitudes. The individual seemed genuinely concerned with trying to help those who have been bullied in life, to see things differently.

I heard on the radio about a 97-year-old couple, who married at 22, and celebrated 75 years of marriage. When asked what kept them together, they both exchanged, "Patience" and "Understanding". There was a pause. And, then she said, "We like to go out and eat together." And, he said, "An occasional cocktail helps."

I also saw an individual post a picture of a sunrise that was spectacular, and did it to make our days brighter. To me, these examples make us a country that is admirable, and on a smaller scale communities where we feel welcome.

In my line of work, I see students who do have trouble with finances. I have been there myself. On a break, one of my students confided that they did not get the books needed as of yet, because they were low on funds, and were awaiting an expected check. I told the person they could borrow mine, since by now, "I should know what is in these publications." We laughed, but another student, patted them on the back, and said, "Let's go down to the bookstore, and I'll cover you, until you get that next check."

That is what makes America outstanding.

Some say you need to handle world affairs, bring in the big bucks, discover a cure for cancer, champion a cause, or sing on a national network to be exceptional. Do not misinterpret me. These are admirable, and I am in no way discounting them. Each of these examples are incredible achievements or other examples of giving back.

But, each day someone is trying to do something simply good for someone else in a simple manner. I am trying to take note, and it helps mold and shape me to be fully aware of the decency that does exist in the U.S. and the world.

Everyday Gifts

A Change Before Our Eyes

Sometimes a person comes into your life, who may need that extra coaching or affirmation. Sometimes what you expect to happen – mysteriously or miraculously changes before your very eyes. At this point in life, I consider these moments, gifts to be experienced and savored. I am grateful for these small miracles.

Be Like a Tea Bag

I walked Como Lake on a beautiful sunny, yet cool, and comforting day. I invariably see many of the same people. There is this one middle-aged lady, with her little dog, walking. Usually, we just say "Good morning", or say something about aches and pains, or how the weather is, and move on. At the end of my circle of the lake, I am just about to head back to my home about five blocks away. I see the woman again on the flip side, and she says: "How many times do you go around?" "Usually, only once." I stopped, and she proceeded to tell me that she has four wonderful kids. And, before I know it she continues to tell me how one of her sons died while roller blading around the lake, and how she was the one who found him. In that moment, I felt her pain, listened, and then asked about her other three kids, and she mentioned how they were all struggling.

I said to her: "Aren't we all? " She proceeded to tell me about her dad, and how he was not very religious and didn't believe in community church, but expressed that "If you take care of your family, you're doing God's will." She remarked how she did not feel strong enough sometimes. I asked her if she knew much about Eleanor Roosevelt. And she said: "I am not that old!" We laughed, and I said, "I am not either, but still found her an amazing source of strength."

I am paraphrasing, but Eleanor said: "Be like a tea bag. You will only find out how strong you are, when you are put in hot water." And, I remarked to the woman with the dog that it sounded like she has been in her share of torrid water.

How many of you are familiar with "Our Lady of Good Remedy"? I was not aware of this affiliation with Mary, the Mother of Jesus, until this morning. But I opened some "junk" mail when I got back home, only to find this particular prayer card, with bonus mailing labels and other religious relics, and such. In the prayer card, it revealed that we should touch other hearts by "bringing comfort to the afflicted and the lonely; help the poor and the hopeless; aid the sick and the suffering." I don't know if this is what happened today in talking with this woman. But she sure reminded me of the gifts I do have in my own life, and to try and step outside of my own life and into another's when the opportunity presents itself.

Engaging the Reluctant

I was in for a morning workout recently, and I searched for a locker. I put my gear on, and a young guy came up to the locker next to mine. I said, "Good Morning." He said "F$%^ off". I was a little startled because I was just waking up and trying to get my own motor running. I paused, and felt my heart beat faster. He was upset. He was throwing stuff out of his gym bag, not violently, but you could tell something was not right.

Before I left, I thought, "Better not engage him anymore." I gave a backwards glance and noticed the man had tears in his eyes as he sat on the small bench in the locker room.

It was very quiet this morning. Something told me not to leave. I turned and said, "I hope it gets better, man." He looked up incredulously and proceeded to tell me that he lost his job, his girlfriend and he were fighting too much, and his car was a piece of sh&*, among other things.

I sat down and listened, but like everyone else, we have to go do the things we do each day. After about 20 minutes, and giving a few encouraging words, and a smile, I took off to do my routine. I am not sure if taking time with this guy made a difference or not. But, it made me realize once again that we, in our own unique ways, have the chance to be here for others on this Earth.

Enamored by the Good

I continue to be enamored by people who are good to others. (You are probably thinking that I need to wake up and look around me). Yes. There are individuals who can do some destructive, hurtful things to others. And, then there are those who make your day.

One individual was Linda, a flight attendant for Delta Airlines, who was present during my flight from Phoenix. You could see that she enjoyed working with passengers, attending to their needs, and handling difficult customers with grace and humor.

People were given a delicious beverage, and their choice of almonds, pretzels, kind bars, or cookies. After consuming this light cuisine, I approached the back of the plane to stretch, to find Linda sitting in a seat juxtaposed tightly between the two restrooms.

I said, "Miss. They should let you wear football pads to prevent bruises!" I noticed a line forming, and the door grazing her legs, and in some cases slamming her, each time people go in and out of these compact lavatories. She laughed, and said, "It comes with the job, but they could have designed this to be more comfortable."

Later, she came back to see how all of us were doing, to insure our flight was enjoyable. When she got to me, she said, "That crunch box you ordered earlier was kind of stale, wasn't it?"

I told her it was just fine. She confided that she also had one, and the Arizona air must have dried out the contents.

"Here are some additional cookies to make up for it", even though I was already satisfied. I thought she was giving me special treatment, but realized that is how she was with all of the passengers, responding to specific needs and their individual situations.

Linda made my day, and the other 169 passengers, too.

Fifty Cents

A woman was buying coffee and developing film at one of those self-serve kiosks at Walgreen's. She was in front of my daughter and myself. I was picking up film that I had developed from a recent trip, and some random shots. It usually takes me months to go through a roll of film. I was excited to see what was on there. At the time, I did not have digital photos, but the old 35 mm camera film. This lady was fumbling through her purse, trying to find the correct amount of money.

"Ten dollars and fifty cents," the cashier said, again.

She didn't have the 50 cents. Every nook and cranny in her purse she scoured.

Then she said, "Oh, yes, I can pay with my credit card!"

The man swiped it. Denied. Inactive card. My daughter and I waited somewhat patiently. While she still searched, I told the man to take my buck and pay for her remainder with that.

The lady said, "I guess I'll have to come back. I live ten miles away. Oh, I guess I should have...."

"Miss, the customer paid for it."

"What?"

"This gentleman paid for it."

The lady paused and sighed. Then, she exclaimed: "Wow! Happy Christmas! I mean, Happy Fourth of July. I mean, Happy the Day After Independence!"

I told her to have a good day. She remarked to the cashier, "You don't see that every day, do ya?"

"No, you don't, miss." He said.

My brother Tom once said to me, "You can't take it with you!" So, losing 50 cents won't hurt me.

Gift of a Stone

There is a story of a wise woman who was traveling in the mountains who found a precious stone in a stream. The next day she met another traveler who was hungry, and the wise woman opened her bag to share her food. The hungry traveler saw the precious stone and asked the woman to give it to him.

Surprisingly, she did so without hesitation. The traveler left, rejoicing in his good fortune. He knew the stone was worth enough to give him security for a lifetime. But a few days later, he came back to return the stone to the wise woman.

"I've been thinking," he said. "I know how valuable the stone is, but I give it back in the hope that you can give me something even more precious.

The wise woman ended with, "Give me what you have within you that enabled you to give me the stone." *from* "The Wise Woman's Stone"

These Peaches are at Their Finest

People are incredible gifts and complex human beings. On a beautiful morning, my good friend, Rita and her congregation graciously welcomed me into the Gardner Grove Baptist Church, where I celebrated joyfully with other members in the Augusta community. I learned from the Pastor that we all have something to be grateful for, and if Goliath gets in your way of reaching your dreams, and you cross the line to face this challenge, you might have to smite this behemoth of a problem, or go around it. "God is great", according to the minister.

Receiving a generous sized jar of grape jelly upon departure, and being welcomed back anytime was a nice way to leave a worship service. I said my goodbye to Rita, gave her a thankful hug, and headed back to where I was staying.

I stopped at a Waffle House, only to discover that one of the waitresses was a "hot wheels" collector, who had over 20,000 miniature cars to her name, and that she actually had scaled back a bit, because she and her family were running out of space at home, and her passion had become an addiction. "My husband doesn't like people much, but at collector shows, he brightens up, and starts conversations with other miniature car enthusiasts." She went on to say, "Hot wheels Inc. makes 575 new models each year, not including all the different colors of each make, so each year I get amped up to check out what's available."

I walked back to the "I've seen better days" Days Inn in Aiken, where I slumbered in the evenings. I witnessed a lady feeling her way along the walls back to the front check-in office, and thought she might be sick, drunk, and/or delirious. I approached her and asked if she was trying to reach the office.

I then realized that she was blind, and walked her back to the front desk, only to find that she works at the front desk, with another associate! Heartily laughing, she said, "Thanks for staying at the Days Inn, and thanks for getting my ass back to where I belong." I surprisingly laughed too, and said, "My pleasure". Arnie, her associate, said: "Sorry about those concrete chunks in the bottom of the pool. We cleaned it up."

The outdoor pool was like stepping into a warm bath, with no typical adjustment period needed to acclimate your body to the water. The day before, while swimming, I felt some hard substances on the bottom of my feet, only to find that it was some kind of disintegrating rock, from the sides of the pool. I removed them one by one, making a game out of it.

Rosemary, another worker, stopped to tell me that the guys next door trashed their room, and favored Lite beers from Miller, for which there were many empty cans all over the floor. I told her that I was not a smoker, but my room had the scent of Marlboros. She said, "That's due to those same guys next door. Smoke comes through the vents. Be careful of those fools."

Later that morning, Edwina, with Rosemary in the background, brought me two peaches the size of grapefruits, and said, "Paul - You come back again! I am headed to church." The day before, she promised she would come back, and delivered them with a smile, "These peaches are at their finest." People are gifts – Yet, we all have complexities, which cannot be fully explained.

Let the Light Emerge

I was thinking of my wife Jan, who explained the best way to start a fire, while sitting out one autumn night. It was cool outside, and so I promised that I would start a fire in the pit in our backyard. I was having a little trouble getting it going, and Jan and the girls came out after watching *How to Succeed in Business without Really Trying*, to detail for me the two methods of fire-making, which included but were not limited to layering sticks separated flat and allowing enough space for air, and the other method of creating a fork of sticks and building a teepee structure.

She says she learned this in the Girl Scouts, in years past. After I let my male ego subside because I couldn't get it to ignite with my own efforts, I watched Jan, and saw how she used a gentle approach, and how her experience and patience made the flame increase its fullness and beauty. I thought of how she was able to get the flame to succeed with her own approach (it didn't seem like she had to try that hard).

We eventually were able to jump start the fire together, as the moisture evaporated in the bottom of the pit, but later I thought of how we as individuals have embers of fire within, which have the potential to create a huge flame for ourselves and others, yet we often do not get the chance or exposure to let our light shine to its full expectations.

I see many of us not feeling like we get our needs met, and others who would like more than what we have been given. If only someone would send a gentle breeze our way, instead of blowing too hard and extinguishing our flame--we might actually burn brighter, and be subjugated to darkness less.

It also occurred to me that I was at first muddling through trying to get the fire going by myself, with the dampness and moist sticks on the bottom of the pit from a previous rain deluge. My efforts took longer than expected, without very good results.

It seems that life can also be like that, where sometimes we feel kind of like smoldering embers that seem drenched in our own problems to such an extent that we somehow cannot continue trying to coax the light to emerge. It is just too hard, and no one will listen. Jan somehow sensed this and helped the fire to blossom. I think we can also do this for one another.

For me, sending a gentle breeze to a good friend, a colleague, or loved one might be just what is needed to jump start their own fire. It could stir up those lingering embers in their own being to create something of beauty and wonder in an individual, which eventually might create some joy for a few, and ultimately goodness for all of us.

Plenty of Goodness Going On

Last week I saw people make the best of a sendoff gathering for a young man who lost his father earlier that same morning while being in a new land - thousands of miles from home. It brought him a joy and comfort he and we will not forget.

Also, the same week, I saw a committee thoughtfully deliberate for a student to succeed in some way, even though he failed on many counts. Constructive care gave him hope.

Yesterday evening, while walking our dog, I saw a young couple sharing moments of affection together, with one giving the other a pat on the back every block, while they progressed forward. Love and affirmation make a difference.

Someone in Your Midst

On a day when I was giving blood, sitting by a colleague who also did the same, we traded friendly quips about his Lions beating my Minnesota team. I lamented that a steak was named "The Viking" - the caption underneath reading, "It has been beaten in 4 superbowls, so it has to be tender." Possibly, giving of ourselves may provide life to another.

While giving blood, I noticed two young women sharing a story where one of the ladies was laughing so hard, that she had tears coming down her face. Laughter heals.

"For I know the plans I have for you," declares the Lord, "plans to prosper you and not to harm you, plans to give you hope and a future" (Jeremiah 29:11).

When a senseless act of loss and life occurs, I, like you, grieve and my heart goes out to the families. Yet, still I haven't given up on humanity. There is plenty of goodness going on. There is an abundance of hope. And, we can help create this hope for the future.

Teamwork

One morning, I brought my daughter and son-in-law to the airport, and stopped at a shop near where they live before pick-up.

I saw twins conjoined - Abby and Brittany. I approached them with some hesitancy. I wanted to give them space. I told them that they had an impact on kids I taught in high school, and how I used their example of tying shoes (when they were 7 years old), with these two sisters doing the thinking to completing this task, and how teamwork and cooperation were so important to this process.

It was a pleasure to meet them, and in our conversation discovered that both of these accomplished young ladies are also teachers.

Who are Your True Heroes?

Have you ever asked yourself who your true heroes are? Maybe it is someone like Plato, who through Socrates' teaching, or as Aristotle's instructor, gave us many of the principles we ponder today, and who changed Western civilization's ways of thinking for many millenniums.

Or maybe, it is Brunelleschi, a brilliant architect, who created the Duomo in Florence, as a master innovator, who influenced Leonardo DaVinci to do many of the great works he is noted for.

Maybe, it was Elizabeth I, whose leadership promoted many of the perspectives that we witness today in Europe.

Or Martin Luther King, who in the effort to promote equality for all people, served selflessly, and eventually gave his life for it.

But, quite possibly, it is someone right in our midst. Turn around. The people who have got your back – your parents and guardians – are true heroes in my mind. They have given you a life that many in this world could only dream of.

Could it be that it is a friend, who has stuck by you, in the most troubling of times, or someone who continually listens to your ideas, and supports you for who you are? A true friend is hard to come by. Respect them.

Maybe, it is a teacher, or someone who believed in you. And gave you the encouragement you needed when you felt like you couldn't expand your essay, or filled in the gaps when it came to tackling an algebra problem, that seemed unsolvable. Or maybe they just wrote you a letter of recommendation for college. Be grateful. Count your blessings.

But, I believe that we need more heroes in our world. The trouble is that we are all somewhat flawed characters. We've got our own troubles, idiosyncrasies, feelings of inadequacy, and sometimes a lack of belief in our own abilities. So, you might say to yourself: "I'm no hero."

I think you are. I think of a young lady in high school who gave her lunch money to someone else, who truly needed the meal. It was apparent that this is all the young lady had for herself, but she wanted the other person to have a chance at lunch that day.

Doing What is Right

We hear a lot of talk about being people of integrity. A good example is the issue of the use of steroids. We've seen many fine athletes jeopardize and possibly ruin their health, just to accelerate their athletic prowess in their sport. Even in the world of table tennis, where I have tried to play my best - I have been offered steroids to enhance my performance. Especially, since I continually get beat on a regular basis. So, it is naturally tempting to try to get an edge somehow.

Well, I have seen the damage that has been done to some of my fellow athletes, and have stayed clear of these substances. Also, it is illegal, and the perception exists that as long as we do not get caught, and you continue to get away with it, keep doing it until you get busted.

Can we as people do things for what is right and just?

You are a Caress of God

Can we take the time to see the beauty and wonder in each other? Our time on this planet is so short. You are a gift and do make a difference.

Many people I encounter, as a teacher, question their value. Pope Francis sings the beauty and value of every living thing - "None is superfluous," and "everything is... a caress of God" no matter how brief its time on earth.

You Have Something to Give and It Can Have an Impact

I have never thought very highly of myself. I guess that makes me a bit insecure. Like all of you, I have individual strengths, and for me, a good number of areas where I fall short. There are so many people who have put me back on the path when I got lost, or guided me when I needed direction.

Or, they have told me where I can have an impact, when I am unsure. I have also seen how we do not give ourselves enough credit for who we are and we may also feel we do not fully measure up.

God made you in a way that no one can fully duplicate. Even identical twins differ in ways of approaching life. But, that in its essence is where beauty lies. You have something to give that someone else has never been able to fully tap. You have the power to share what you have been blessed and given, with someone who needs your skill set.

Realize the person in front of you, or beside you, or at your back puts on their pants one leg at a time. (If you don't wear pants, this story may have little meaning for you). My point is we are all human beings, all trying to get by with our own bags of phenomenal attributes, some bad memories and experiences, but so much more to offer each other. You may not fully realize your indelible impact on the person who you just met, or is in your presence right now.

Everyday Life

Accident in the Supershuttle

I boarded the Supershuttle to the Pittsburgh Airport. The driver insisted that seatbelts need to be fastened before he proceeded. I happened to board first and he had to pick up two other customers. The first individual after me was a young guy half asleep.

The last person was a lady who was being picked up at her apartment. After a short delay she approach the van and was having a small fit. I turned to check my carryon bag and before you know it, somehow the lady threw her own bag in the backseat. The handle got stuck in my shoulder seatbelt (quit laughing) and pulled my head back a bit violently.

The young guy was now awake and said, "Dude that had to hurt". The lady who lassoed me was very quiet and nodded an apology. Who knew you could get a minor whiplash in the Supershuttle?

Au Naturel

One morning I went to workout to start my day. I hit the showers early, and a man starts telling me that he must have been the first one in here, because the water was running cold, and he explained how it eventually became warm after waiting for a while. I thanked him for the info, and the next thing you know, he followed me out telling me about his life while being "naked, unclothed, undressed, disrobed, stripped, unclad, without a stitch on", into the community men and women's lobby by accident, on the way to the pool.

I said, "Whoa! You may want to turn around. People will see you."

He was startled, and said that he usually doesn't come to this club, and he sometimes gets mixed up, and goes through the wrong doors.

Did I mention that this guy almost went commando, in his "au naturel birthday suit" into the community pool area? I imagined the screams that might have followed upon full entry into the pool area.

Bad to Worse

You ever have those mornings where things can suddenly go from bad to worse? I can't say mine was starting off badly. I went to get some donuts for my veteran physical therapy colleagues, where I volunteer in transport. Being an overcast day, I thought I would try to brighten my mood and others with sugar.

Something that I noticed is that when the barometric pressure changes, mood can change. I thought this pressure could have influenced what happened to me this morning. My first vet to pick up, started screaming at me and threatened to kick my a$$ out if I didn't leave immediately. He had some issue with his wheelchair from a previous day, and said that everyone had lied to him. I didn't know the context, but he wanted his comfortable chair back. I told him that Kate was expecting him for therapy, and he emphatically told me with a series of expletives that he didn't give a s$%^ who wanted him, that he is not going and to "get the hell out." I told him that I was disappointed that he couldn't go down for therapy, and that hopefully his morning gets better.

This volunteer job of four plus years has taught me some resilience, patience, the ability to listen under fire, and that not everything is going to go as smoothly as we hope.

Also, what we see on the surface of a person is not always the full story. In the Leadership program at Saint Mary's, we talk about and practice building a better sense of self-awareness, self-regulation, motivation, empathy and social skills. In this instance, my motivation was already strong to work with the individuals who have served our country.

But, I must admit that I had to do everything in my power to self-regulate my reactions, empathize with this individual's pain and frustration, have the self-awareness to realize that I have limits to how much I am going to give and take, and the social skills to communicate to the designated veteran psychologist what happened.

I realized after this meeting that this veteran had some leftover shrapnel in his hip that caused severe pain. No wonder he was upset.

Now I Understand

At the Vet's Home, I had an active day of taking people back and forth from their rooms and nursing stations to physical therapy. I truly enjoy it, and get to know some of our veterans and their stories. One of our men, who served in Vietnam and was wounded in action, was so upset today that it felt like fire was coming out of his mouth and ears.

He was yelling at staff. As a volunteer, it was my turn to bring him back from physical therapy. "You better not leave me in the hallway!" I said to him, "You are a war hero, with a Purple Heart. I will make sure you get back to your room. Thanks for your service, my friend."

"Damn right you will, you son of a b&@$h!". At this point I was not in a position to play this game this morning or deal with this. But, it is not uncommon to feel the wrath, because many of these individuals do have many pains for a variety of reasons, so I take it in stride. I said, "Look, my friend. You are in good hands. I will get you back safely to your room. But, I am not going to deal with your anger today." He looked at me kind of quizzically, paused, and said, "Son. You have no idea what I saw each day where I was stationed." And then, he settled down. As we got back to his room, on the wall, were pictures of those friends he lost in the Southeast Asian conflict - and it helped me understand a little bit more.

Occasionally I am Nice

Another time, I encountered a notable individual on my shift. This man announces proudly that he is 95 years old, as I push him from physical rehabilitation to his room.

I asked him, "Did you get to this milestone by living the life of an optimist?"

He stated proudly,

"No, I have been a mean son of a ^&*%$ all my life, and occasionally I am nice. That's my secret." Meanwhile on the trek back to getting other rehab folks, one vet asked me if I have any toothpicks; another asked if I can secure him some smokes; a nurse notifies one

17

of the residents that they have choir practice this morning, and then he let's everyone know on his floor - "I can't sing a note, but need someone to help me to the restroom. It better be fast!"

Such is life.... I admire the nurses, staff, and rehabilitation workers that do their jobs each day to help make these veterans lives better.

The Little Guy Wants to Be Included

At times, we have questions from our advisees on what direction to take with course load for each semester. One student admitted in her email that she was rather stressed. I decided to call this individual and problem solve on the phone. The conversation started out well, but all of a sudden her son started to cry, scream, and fuss.

He wanted his mom. She was trying to balance her attention with me and the little tike.

She apologized, and I explained that my kids at one time were like this, and "Now that they are full fledged adults, I cry and fuss around them." She laughed.

The little boy was not relenting, and I asked if I could talk with him. The woman put him on the phone, and I said, "Your momma needs to finish this so she can take care of you soon." This little two year old probably didn't understand a word I was saying, but, gurgled, and said, "Doh. Dey." And, he temporarily quieted down so we could finish the advisory process. I said to the woman that "he just wanted to be part of her education plan!"

Being a Dad

I would like to think I know what I am doing as a dad. But, in reality, I make a lot of mistakes and I don't know if my efforts make a difference. But, I do know that I love my kids, and this counts for something. Here's to all the dads, guardians and mentors out there who pick up young people when they fall; and celebrate their kids when they do something right.

Being in A Rut

Someone sent me a note about being in a "rut". You ever get in a rut? Stuck on the merry-go-round of a bad habit? I have. You are going to make mistakes. I have found that I need to own them, make amends, and move on.

Guilt and regret kills many a man and woman before their time. Turn the page, get off the ride. YOU are the author of the book of your life. Turn the page and do try something else that's positive.

Dust Your Shoes off and Try Again

I was reflecting on Leonardo da Vinci, who was often told to cater and ingratiate himself with those in Florence, who had the finances, such as the de Medici family and others. Lorenzo of this same family, kept Leonardo out of consideration for major architectural projects, including painting the Sistine Chapel, for a variety of reasons in addition to jealousy. Leonardo wasn't considered as literary, but more scientific. He was illegitimate, and as a result, not allowed in elite universities and barred from noble professions.

He even created plans and a clay sculpture of a horse the size of a building, to eventually be cast in bronze. Unfortunately, war broke out and all the metal was needed for battle, and so his work was criticized for coming to nothing.

But, still he persisted in trying to understand the essence of life itself, and eventually created ideas for flight, large-scale architecture, and key findings in anatomy. So, when someone tells you are not capable, or not worthy, find a new avenue to walk down and create something extraordinary.

Each Day is Precious - I'll Never Forget 911

I'll never forget 9/11/2001. It was my second year in the classroom of a secondary high school, and I was teaching Geometry at the time.

I thought I was in the middle of a refreshing teaching lesson, where sophomores were making 3-D tetrahedrons and describing the angle properties, and relationships between sides and angles. We had scissors and paper everywhere, and students were in a pretty convivial mood.

That aside, somewhere between 9 and 9:30 AM, our principal came on the P.A. and announced that we could turn on our TV's. In a calm voice, she announced that an airplane had hit the World Trade Center.

I am not sure if we even knew at that time, that it was a terrorist attack.

I turned on my TV monitor, my heart racing. We saw the footage (Was it CNN or Fox?), and one kid said, "That is so cool. Can we see that again?" After explaining that lives were being lost, the kid recoiled, and felt somewhat ashamed.

Two other students were in tears, mainly because they knew their parents might possibly be in the airplane that crashed. Some students wanted to pull out cell phones. All of us were stunned in our own ways. And for a teenager, I don't know what would go through my mind. Keeping them calm, and patient was quite a chore in itself (as I am sure you remember), where you were and what you were doing at the time.

As has been said many times, "This day changed me."

Each day to me is invaluable. And this day still stirs up emotions.

I realize today once again, how lucky we are to have people who give of their time and in many instances their lives for our freedom. I also cannot take for granted that each day is a gift, so we should live it to the fullest.

Funeral Talk in the Hot Tub

Occasionally, I struggle with some arm pain, so I went to workout and then sat in the hot tub. A gregarious guy started talking to me about the Twins having a great start of the season, the nice weather, and then he asked me point blank: "Have you prepared for your funeral, burial plot, and the possibility of cremation?"

I was a bit taken aback, never discussing death seriously in a whirlpool setting. At the time, I was working on my elbow, with one of the jets, and he proceeded to tell me about his work, and that he helps people prepare for the inevitable. I am thinking to myself, "People are dying to talk to you!"

Approaching people in the hot tub seems like a great new way to market funeral and burial services.

I Am Not that Young

Every year there is a volunteer appreciation luncheon at the Minneapolis Veteran's Home. A lady from the reception area approached me as I entered the food service line, and said, "Young man, this lunch is for the volunteers. Guests have to pay a fee. Thank you for understanding." It just so happens that I do volunteer there (as you may have noticed from prior stories - once a week), and the great majority of the attendees for this lunch are 65+, so I smiled, and someone eventually vouched for me, and asked why I wasn't working at this time of day.

I had to explain that I teach at night, and this fit into my schedule. And, that being with the veterans is something I truly enjoy. I will not complain about being perceived as too young. Someday this will no longer happen.

Elvis Has Left the Building Again

I bought tickets for Jan and I to see an impersonator at the former Las Vegas Hilton for a Friday night. He was to perform as "Elvis".

It was very quiet. We sat in the Shimmer Showroom for about 20 minutes, when a manager asked us if we needed some help.

"We are here to see the Elvis show!" He explained that the show had been cancelled, and a note was sent to all ticket holders via email.

Somehow he decided not to show up this night.

Elvis had literally left the building. It was kind of disappointing. We were really looking forward to this event in the Shimmer Showroom. Apparently, he stayed in Florida, with the Neil Diamond impersonator.

Find a New Hubby

I was half awake on a morning drive. As I was passing a local community education center, I thought I saw a sign that said: "Find a New Hubby". Underneath, it said: "56 New Classes". I was a bit astounded, thinking one class should be sufficient, if that.

I eventually realized that the first line said: "Find a New Hobby". I should get my eyes checked.

Determination versus Common Sense

"Sears, where America goes for value!" That's what my wife and I did, after having a nice ride on a Saturday in June. My wife asked if I want to go shop.

"What's at Sears?"

"I just want to look around for clothes. Work clothes."

After hemming and hawing in my own mind, knowing full well that we were spending time together, intermixed with reading the paper, I took note of her courtesy toward me, and then decided to reciprocate.

"Sure, honey." It was 1:30 pm. "Let's meet back here."

"Near the table with boxes that have little dots on them? How about at 2:00?"

"2:15, I need to try on stuff, while you look at tools."

She assumed I wanted to look at tools. I have enough tools to keep any guy happy with fixing things.

"All right, I'll meet you back here at 2:15," I said.

So off to my own adventure. I don't go to the tools section, but find amazing deals on shirts and shorts. It is Summer. I try on some clothes. "6 items maximum allowed in fitting rooms".

Clothes don't fit you well in your 40's. Okay, well not in my own eyes on my own body. But, I find this wonderful shirt "Linen", my wife has said in the past.

"It wrinkles easy." I pay for my clothes. The lady at the counter says "It's hot in here." I said, "I was just outside. It feels pretty good to me. But, you work in here. Probably been here a while, huh?"

"Yeah."

Well, I depart from the affable employee who is feeling overheated, assuming that my pair of shorts, and two shirts have been cleared of security tags, but when I check the next morning, Sunday, realize that one of them still has the security tag still on the sleeve.

I wanted to wear this new shirt to go out with my wife, who like me wanted to spend more time outdoors. So we called my brother who decided to join us. No problem. I notice before we go that the plastic clamp is stuck to the sleeve of my new shirt.

"Aren't they supposed to take these off?! It says, "Do not remove without a sales attendant's help, or ink may damage the clothes. Aw! Why now?"

My wife notices my frustration, and says you'll just have to take that shirt back to Sears", with a little chuckle. Also, "Linen", my wife says. "It wrinkles easy."

It's probably a guy thing. But, it is Sunday morning. I want to wear this shirt. So, I say to myself, is it worth driving all the way to Sears and not wanting to see the sales attendant tell me how overheated she is, and "Sir, do you have your receipt?" and trying to explain that I didn't steal this…when I could probably have taken this off myself.

"Don't do that Pauly. You'll ruin the shirt. I wouldn't do that." Said my wise wife.

She was right, but I was determined. Sure enough, there I am, while my wife has just ascended the stairs from her shower, looking out the window, going "Oh my God! You're not using a hacksaw are you?"

"Yes, I am."

"Guys! Can't you just drive to Sears to return it?! You're going to ruin your shirt."

Well I'm going to do this. Got to show I have some skills that make me a man. It has a metal fastener that is made of metal, which prevents one from trying to pull it apart, by normal means, as you might have guessed.

So the hacksaw seemed to make sense. Was there ink in there? Yes. Did I avoid getting it on the shirt? Yes, this time. But in the process, I added a rust stain from the hacksaw to the shirt. I flushed the stain with some water, and I was good to go. Sometimes determination outweighs common sense.

Marriage Takes Work

Marriage takes work. There is no doubt about it. I have been lucky. Sometimes the stars align, and God gives you someone who challenges you, makes you better, complements your weaknesses with their strengths, and serves as your friend.

Laughter and seeing that tomorrow is another day, realizing that not getting what you want can be a stroke of luck, and realizing that you just do not have all the answers, (but that your wife often does), has given me many blessings along the way.

Plus, a good friend suggested that forgiveness - living by the rule of "7 times 70", which she explained means that "we need to forgive this many times before rushing to judgment." I am still working on this one, but it is fitting advice.

I Love Hash Browns

Recently, I went through a White Castle drive-thru for breakfast, with the intention of giving the same cuisine I ordered to someone who could use a morning "pick me up". I selected two delicious "egg and cheese on a bun" sandwiches, strong coffee, and small cinnamon cake donuts.

So, I thought I was equipped with two identical breakfasts, and planned to give one of these combinations to the first individual with a "will work for food" sign, or something like it. Some of you are thinking "Why would you ever go to this place for breakfast?!"

My route through Minneapolis gives me more than my share of these opportunities. Instead, everyone was apparently sleeping or taking a break this morning, so I gave it to one of our dedicated security guards when I arrived at work.

He accepted the coffee, opened the bag with a thank you, and said, "Jesus! I love hash browns." I didn't remember ordering the quarter-sized hash browns, but the White Castle staff somehow added this unintended bonus for my security guard friend, miraculously including the ordered items, too! I on the other hand, enjoyed the cinnamon cake donuts with coffee.

When You Decide to Give Things Just Show Up

I was driving one morning, and noticed I was short on gas. I thought before I filled my tank …."I will pick up some breakfast at McDonald's." I decided to buy a McMuffin combo, with the classic potato cake and coffee. As I proceeded to the drive thru, I thought, "You only need a McMuffin." So, I ordered the combo and another McMuffin, thinking…"I am going to give this combo to the first person I see today, who could use a breakfast." I find a gas station, with my combo meal on the passenger seat.

I already devoured the one sandwich. I proceeded to pay at the pump, thinking I will give this breakfast to the gas attendant. I caught the attendant's eye from outside, while filling the tank, and showed the bag to him, which said: "I'm Lovin' It". He looked away.

I entered and said: "Could you use a breakfast this morning? McMuffin, potato cake, and coffee, with crème?" He gave me an astonished look, and I said, "I think I know you." He said: "Sure, I'll take this! Thanks." It just so happens this young man had worked in our yard with some landscaping, a year ago, and subsequently had to make a trip to a southern state to reunite with his estranged wife and children.

We talked a bit, as he recognized me from the past. We laughed about the past, and he proceeded to say his life was not going so well, and the relationship he hoped to unify fell apart. I reassured him and mentioned that it always stings when you break up, and have to start anew. We exchanged numbers, and I hoped to help find this guy some work he enjoys.

As I left, tears came to his eyes, and I told him to "Never give up.

It will get better, and you will heal." I discussed this with my wife, Jan, and she said: "When you decide to give, things just show up." There is power in just simple acts.

Miles to Go

One morning, in a parking lot, placed on a street lamp foundation, were a pair of shoes. They looked like a Fubu brand; they were quite stylish, and were also soaking wet from the recent deluge of rain.

I wondered whether someone forgot them after a workout, left them on purpose, or maybe started a different path in life without these shoes. These high tops still had some good tread on them. So, I brought them in and placed them on a mat inside the building, so someone could claim them after they dried off. Maybe, someone else would place dibs on them or set them in motion. These pumps had some life that needed some additional mileage before they became obsolete from a worn out stride and sole.

These empty shoes are a symbol of the freedom we have. If you are able bodied, you have the power to do just about anything or go anywhere you want. Without shoes, you can make it barefoot for a while, but, in this society, you may be limited in your groundwork. Your shoes can take you on an exciting journey, start a new path, or could be placed in a repository until you are ready to use them again.

I am not sure where these shoes will end up, but I think they, like all of us, have some additional miles to go before they sleep.

Opening up the Conversation

Jake (our dog) and I were walking in the Como area. It is a peculiar thing when you have a canine, how some people become very social with you, not necessarily because they want to talk to you, but because they want to greet, play, pet your dog, or tell you about their experiences with owning a pet. There is no doubt in my mind that it is another avenue for opening up a conversation.

We were passing up a lady having a smoke, and she turned around eagerly, and was so enamored by Jake. He greeted her by jumping up and down, and I explained the usual: What kind of dog he is, his age, the fact that he has the energy to drag me around the lake, his sociability, and that I got this pup as a present for my wife.

The lady then said, "Sir. I thought you were blind, and the little guy is your seeing eye dog. I wasn't sure." Thank you for Ray Bans.

I laughed and said: "Well, there are some days I feel like I am walking blind in life. But, it is all good."

Who Wears the Pants in Your Family?

Someone once said that "luck is the thing that draws us for jury duty, but never for the lottery." This morning on a walk toward the zoo, a man in a Como area parking lot, wearing Hawaiian shorts, and shirtless, sees me approach with our little dog, Jake, and starts laughing hysterically. Mind you it was at us. "Was that your wife's idea?!" "Who wears the pants in your family?! Ah Ha!"

As I am used to these encounters. (I am tall and this is a very short little Bichon/Shih-Tzu).

I thought to myself, "Where is your shirt, and what is up with the shorts?" But, instead, I said, "You look like you are ready for a party? It's a little early, isn't it, dude?"

After a little more banter, and realizing this guy was innocuous, he proceeded to tell me he was a drifter, who lives in Florida half the year and Minnesota the other.

"I love Minnesota! Water is free. Lots of parks, plenty of places to sleep!" Even with his bold laugh, his eyes showed some weariness from daily life. He was very entertaining, and as we departed company, this man with his can of half eaten Dinty Moore stew left me thinking - I am lucky. I haven't won a lottery, but the connection with this man was a moment of unexpected surprise, maybe luck, and some joy. I have to admit, I do look funny with this little dog.

Potent Beers

One night, I headed out to the Bauhaus to try out some craft beers and celebrate a friend's birthday. Mind you, I only had two of these delicious beverages, but they do have a bit of potency at 6.5% (Wagon Train) and 7.4% (Sky Five). It was a great time of laughter and camaraderie. I then went home, hit the sack, and I had kind of a teacher's nightmare. In the dream....

I was just hired to teach a new organizational effectiveness course, at a new college. Somehow, I got stuck in traffic, even though I left an hour and a half in advance of class. I couldn't find the building, or the room, and I asked a young college student if they could help me find my destination, and they said, "I'm busy." The kid was smoking a hookah pipe.

I finally made it to my assigned course, and my class list had 43 students. When I entered the room, there were students jumping on trampolines; gymnasts doing somersaults and cartwheels; people giving me blank stares and asking me if I was the new teacher (The last one was eaten by the alligator); livestock walking freely through the room such as mooing cows with yellow ribbons on their heads, and a group of monkeys playing cards in the back of the room. I also wasn't able to turn the computer on.

To top it off there was a screaming goat, who wasn't holding back. I am so glad I woke up at 5:30 am this morning to realize this was just a nightmarish dream....

Scams and Acting

As I took the 7th Street exit from 94, and turned left on 11th Avenue, a construction worker with hardhat and reflective vest approached my moving car and asked me to stop.

He asked if I would give his family waiting in the parking lot on 8th Street some bus fare. He claimed that he had to go to work, and didn't have time to get the money to his family. I said, "I will see what I can do." He then interjected immediately and said, "If you give the money to me, I can get them on the bus myself, but I might be late." Then, it occurred to me that it was a bold impersonation scam, yet a creative one at that! This guy had the costume for the role, too. Acting!

Searching for the Smile

At Dale Street exit and 94, a tall gaunt man had a sign that said "Anything Helps." My latest small gift while waiting for the light is to give people (who are struggling) my favorite gum. I usually give two pieces. Other times, I give out fortune cookies, and wish these folks "a better day," and to hang in there. The man I gave the gum to said to me that I was "the first person who talked to him today and also gave him something."

He started dancing joyously a bit, and said "Thanks". I have seen tears and an occasional outburst of anger, on other days of the week. Some people say that one of these times I am going to get punched in the face, or worse. But, I have to say it is that smile, or glimmer of hope I am seeking.

Second Chances

I was just thinking about second chances. In my life, I have seen countless examples of people who have seen the errors of their own ways, rebound, reshape positively, and make a difference in the world. I am thankful to those who helped me grow along the way. There are plenty of areas in our world where we can be critical of what we are not doing well in this world.

But, each day, I find incredibly talented, well-intentioned people who do help others by leading, coaching others to reach their goals, and intentionally picking up those who drop into a major abyss and need a hand up to get back on track in their lives. Thank you for being there.

Tarragon for a Pie

One day, my wife told me about her work at a floral shop and revealed a story of an older woman with a smile that could provide enough energy for all of St. Paul's lighting needs. It all started when the lady pulled Jan's ponytail, (which she likes to wear, because it's practical, functional, and looks good on her - as long as it is not too tight).

After the unexpected pull, Jan turned around, and that same lady with a radiant smile that didn't diminish, said, "Can you tell me if you have any Tarragon?"

Jan, as a customer service professional says, "Hmm, let me check for you." It just so happened that after checking, they did not, but the lady was still smiling.

Jan continued: "If we get any in, we could give you a call." The lady explained that she was from out of town. "Maybe I could bring it up to you," Jan cheerfully shot back.

"If and when you do, I'll bake you a pie.", the pint-sized lady gleefully gave back. Jan sounded delighted by this. Maybe we'll make a special delivery of tarragon, and come hope with pastry. People often respond well to kindness.

You are Asking for Trouble Getting on this Elevator

I have never truly taken the time to see the inside of Mayo Clinic in Rochester. Within the walls of this structure, while waiting for an elevator, I was observing a massive sculpture by August Rodin, when a lady being pushed in a wheelchair, and accompanied by two other individuals, says to me, affably, "If you get on this elevator with us, you are asking for trouble and will be taking your chances!"

I said, "Next elevator, please!". She and her friends laughed, and I got on anyway. She then proceeded to ask me if I was bigger than 6' 7" tall, and I told her, "Not even close. I was 6' 2" at one time, and am shrinking a bit with age."

She chortled and eagerly told me all of her brothers and sisters were very tall, and thought I was at least the same height. As they reached their floor at the cancer center, being whisked off the elevator, she said, "I could have sworn that guy was at least 6' 7" tall!"

One of her escorts said, "You're in a wheelchair! Of course he looks bigger."

Growing Up

Beauty and the Beast

To be a dad with daughters is a gift. Not always an easy gift, but one I would never want to trade away or dispense with. My daughters mean so much to me, that I could never fully describe. Small vignettes of time together from the past stay in my mind: Having my 4 and 2 year old girls being afraid of the creature in "Beauty and the Beast", wanting to leave the theater crying (with a bit of screaming), only to find that they too, would eventually find there is good in this mammal, and remaining until the end of the movie, until they realized it; or driving and connecting them to their dad's rock and roll music (albeit from the 60's through the 90's) and seeing both girls appreciate at least some of my taste for an edgy beat.

Both episodes in time, let me know I could give them something not material, but connected with feeling, emotion and the heart. I am grateful for these flashback memories, where now the girls have become women, and individuals who are making their own contributions and way in this world.

Bright Eyed Kids

I thought I heard our mailbox open one evening, and looked outside the window to see two bright-eyed grade school girls moving to the next house.

They saw me in the window, and u-turned to knock on our door eagerly again, and tag teamed me with: "Sir, we have two kinds of items for you to buy for our fundraiser. We have food items and ribbons." The food items looked pretty enticing, yet soups were $17.00, and cookies and candy items were around $13.00. "We have lot of items for Christmas, and the holidays."

I told them I would focus on the food items and chose the beer batter bread, for a modest price. "Thanks for not shutting the door on us", the one young lady said. The other girl said, "Yeah. No one has opened the door for us, yet." (I am thinking to myself that I am sorry I opened the door, because it's going to cost me!) Yet, I thought back to when I was a kid, and gave in to buy the beer batter bread, plus we gave the two young ladies some credit for being good salespeople.

That night, I received a phone call from a mom who thanked me for coaching her son for a chapter of time, who had been bullied so badly in grade school and high school that he didn't want to go back, and didn't. He couldn't take the taunting, humiliation, and painful reminders of his perceived inadequacies from other kids who, were probably hurting inside, and decided to take it out on someone else.

Well, this kid went back to school and went on to college, is doing very well, and is a confident young man, who is now coaching other young people.

One of my favorite quotes that I hung in my classroom, came from George Washington Carver: "How far you go in life depends on you being tender with the young, compassionate with the aged, sympathetic with the striving and tolerant of the weak and the strong. Because someday in life you will have been all of these."

Do You Think You Can Take Him?

I think back to my days as a boy in New York, where, my mom encouraged me as a new kid to go out and play with some of the neighborhood kids. We lived in Amherst, outside of Buffalo, and there were pickup games of football and baseball. I'll never forget being this seven year old, and feeling a little apprehensive to go out and meet kids I've never seen before. With a little cajoling, I embarked on trying to join a baseball game already in progress. Also, my mom had her hands full with a 5 year-old, 4 year-old, and newborn, and needed a break.

"Hey, do you want to play?" I was shy and eager to fit in, but happy someone asked me. "That team is short a player. Join them." The team was batting, and it was my turn. This was kind of a slow pitch version of baseball, but I managed to hit a single and stood kind of proud on first base.

The same kid who invited me was playing at first, and asked me: "See that kid at third base? Do you think you can take him?"

I innocently said: "Take him where?"

"No kid. Do you think you can take him?"

And, I said again, "Take him where?" He said "No, no, no. Do you think you can take him in a fight?" My first time out with this group of guys, and I am presented with a difficult question.

"I don't want to fight anybody. I just want to play ball."

"Come on. Don't you think you could?" Peer pressure gave in, and one of my biggest mistakes, of many I've made in life was to say: "I guess so."

Big Mistake. The guy yells out to the third baseman, "Hey, Jimmy. This guy thinks he can take you!" Before I knew it, I was getting beat-up. I am getting punched mercilessly, and afterward, with a bloody lip, and lots of tears, I thought "Why did I even venture to the playground?!"

I came home in tears and my pride shot, but didn't make as big a deal of it, as maybe I should have. My mom had plenty of young kids to deal with besides me.

After my pummeling incident, an older kid in the neighborhood saw I had been injured, and gave me some ideas on how to interact with others in the neighborhood, protect myself in a fight, and have a sense of humor. He also told me to "use my words a bit more carefully." It let me once again realize that people may not tell you directly, but your words and actions truly can make a difference in people's lives. I am thankful for that older kid, who instilled courage in me to go back to that ballpark with my head held high, and take another swing.

Character

It's something that develops in you from the day you are born. I have seen a lot in my days. Some miracles, some heartbreak, and some joyous events that bring you back for more of the same.

The year in 2008 was particularly difficult. I witnessed some young ladies who had trouble with chemicals and drugs. I also saw some guys who felt compelled to assert their physical prowess and encourage fights. I saw another young lady, whose confidence increased in increments throughout the year, and developed into a wonderful young adult who will do good things in life.

I was struck by the lack of gratitude that some people have, and the sense of entitlement that some of our young people possess. Many people go out of their way to make their experience in high school a memorable one, but it seems to be expected. But, we have all been young.

I have witnessed many cases of apathy, disrespect, and lack of gratitude for what we have been given.

Is character a trait that we are lacking as a society? By Webster's definition, no. We all have something that makes us unique. But, are the unique qualities we possess benefiting society?

Are we developing a character that we can be proud of?

Are we treating each other with the 3R's: respect for one another, respect for ourselves, and responsibility for our actions?

From the Mouth of Babes

My nephew was with us on New Year's Eve. My sister and her husband went out to celebrate with friends. We watched part of Mr. Magoo's Christmas. I told the very young lad that it was time to get his pajamas on.

After we finished getting into sleeping gear, he wanted to finish the show and said: "Uncle Pauly, can we watch Mr. Baggoo's Christmas?!"

I said, "Sure we can."

There is a little boy in the show who is on crutches named Tiny Tim. My nephew at his 2 years and 11 month stage in life said: "Does he need medication?"

I said: "Yes, he probably does."

The youngster said: "Do you like medication?"

"No, not really...."

My nephew said: "I don't either." ....and empathetically, he said, "None of us do."

Pretty good for a kid ready to turn 3.

I Can't Open My Locker

Each year teaching high school, I received a new "homeroom". Here they get news, and have a safe sanctuary to do homework, or talk - the latter is usually the case. I had a young lady, whose locker was continually getting stuck. They have combination locks with three numbers.

You could see tears welling up in her eyes, and she was rather shy, so I asked her what was wrong. She said she could not get her locker open.

So, I left my homeroom temporarily unattended, and said I would be back. We walked across the skyway to the M building, and I asked her to tell me the combination, and promised I wouldn't raid her locker unnecessarily, unless she had some additional snacks.

She wasn't smiling. I had to remind her I was just kidding. I would do my best to get it open.

And then I said, "Okay, now you try Meagan." She missed it. "You have to be careful on that second number. Make one full turn, and then, be right on the tick mark. Try again."

She tried. And opened it. Her tears were drying up. Here's a Kleenex.

"Thanks," she said.

"Now try it a couple more times, and I'll observe. No pressure. Just making sure you can do it. I know you can."

Success! She could do it. It has to be uncomfortable as a freshman in high school, when you can't get your locker open. It's bad enough that kids can be so mean and self-centered to the point of no return and sometimes-sheer terror for some kids. "Let's go back to homeroom," I said.

We walked back and I proceeded to tell her how when I was a freshman, someone learned my combination either looking over my shoulder, or because I was too naïve to cover up my turns of the lock.

Remember that at one time, the lock was not a physical attachment to the locker. You had to bring your own. Anyway, I couldn't get into my locker. The young girl started to smile, and then laugh.

"So you think that's funny, eh? Back then, it wasn't too funny." But, I realized that she and I had been in the same boat. Feeling lost, feeling a little ashamed, and realizing that you may not have anyone to help you.

I reflected back to the kid who did that to me. I was clueless at the time, for at least three days. It always seems longer. I couldn't get into my locker. I had excuses for the teacher, and had to go to see the head maintenance guy, who told me they routinely cut locks off on Saturdays.

This happened on a Tuesday or Wednesday, so either way I would have to make some accommodations. Otherwise, I would be way behind. Some teachers were nice, and let me borrow a book. I was able to get some new notebooks, but it was a hassle.

Routinely throughout the week, the "Rascal", whose name has been changed to protect the innocent (guilty) - Rascal would shout out, "Hey Kotz, can't get into your locker yet? You must be illiterate." "Or hey Kotz, go see the learning specialist."

Anyway, I finally figured out who was responsible, but didn't want to rat him out, because that wouldn't be cool, and I'd be perceived as a crybaby.

I wouldn't have used the word "perceived" at that time. I don't think I knew what that meant. What I found out later, is that he learned my combo, took it off, and put on another lock. I asked him once, if he would give me the combination, and my original lock back, but it never happened. But, it did make me more resilient to those who bullied. I also had to be more careful.

I resolved in this moment that I wouldn't want that to happen to another kid. Thus, we return back to the classroom, and the freshman girl was still smiling as I returned from my flashback to the present. The bell went off. Homeroom was over.

Last Day on the Job

My last day of being a teacher of secondary students was difficult – My room was being painted for the new teacher, and files I wanted to save were removed from my drawers. I had accepted a new job offer.

Two of my favorite maintenance staff were listening to Spanish music, and working their painting magic on the room. One of my colleagues was rummaging through my files. It's all part of change. It's hard to let go of something you truly believe in, yet know in your heart that it is time to shake it up a bit and face up to change.

As I cleaned out my room of my high school experience, over a period of three days (13 years is a long time to accumulate stuff and memories), I found pictures, geometric shapes, great curriculum for AP Stat students, ideas that didn't work as intended; pictures of students who went through incredible struggles, yet somehow managed to make it to adulthood; stories of teenage trials and triumphs, poems, letters, and motivational articles, and many more indelible memories.

I wish I could fully convey to you in words how much I enjoyed teaching high school. As educators and mentors, these teenagers become adults before our very eyes, and it is a stunning gift to witness. Miracles happen and you get to witness it.

My Brother takes AP

Often I would hear kids talk about others in the hallway. I have got to stop listening before I get ready for class.

I was listening to two girls. One said: "You should really take an AP Class."

The other young lady said, "I don't know if I can handle it."

The first young lady remarked: "Well, my brother is taking one now. He's doing very well. And, he's an idiot!"

Ouch. I didn't say all high school kids are kind. Their cerebral cortex is still being fully developed.

I Couldn't Get Out of the Box

Some of you wake up each day, from a position of self-assurance. I am generally known to have a positive personality, but believe me when I say, it is often fraught with self-doubt, uncertainty and sometimes fear for what my next move will be.

I had this dream, where I was asked to play golf with a group of friends. We drew straws, and I was the last one to approach the tee. We were on this platform within a box, and each golfer had to send a shot through this narrow window to reach the fairway.

In this dream, all of the other golfers seemed to manage getting through the window on their tee shot. When it came time for me to swing away, I would continually hit the inside of the shack, the ball would ricochet, people would duck, and eventually run out of the box.

One of the guys was nice enough to say, "Give him a mulligan, and let him try again!" The rest scurried out of the box and observed from outside. Well, as some of you can imagine, I kept trying but couldn't get out of the box.

Initially, I was afraid for my colleagues - for pegging someone, fear of causing a concussion or something far worse. In reality, I have a wicked slice shot, where it wouldn't matter in this dream. I couldn't get out of this rut.

Eventually, everyone gave up on me and kept moving forward to their next shots.

And, then, I woke up! I am sure glad that this was not reality.

Have you ever tried to reconstruct why you are having these dreams? I sometimes try, but usually let it go, forget or move on with the day at hand.

But, it occurred to me that with everyday responsibilities, come everyday hurdles, obstacles, and challenges.

Sometimes, with a dream such as the one I had, I have to step back and say, "You are human. You, too will get stuck in your own rut or box every so often, and may need to re-evaluate your own self-doubt, uncertainty and sometimes fear for a few things in your own life." It is a certainly a journey in life to face all of our daily encounters, in our own ways.

Rudderless

It was a beautiful Sunday, but one that troubled me. My wife and I took the bus to see the Twins baseball team. We often take the 3A bus.

It is a scenic ride through Como Park and Minneapolis, and definitely beats finding parking for sporting events.

What troubled me was the ride home. I was initially concerned about this man who boarded in Minneapolis en route to St. Paul, who immediately passed out on three seats in the front of the bus. I instead decided to focus on a nice conversation with my wife.

Then, in a spontaneous frenzy as we arrived back in the Como area, thirteen kids boarded the bus in a swarm, and the head king pin announces that none of them have their bus cards. They all jump on the bus with a few swearing, and yelling that this is an easy bus to board without paying.

The leader of the group said, "I got you all on for free! Wouldn't happen with that other driver." Then, he looked at my wife and myself and said, "Oh, sorry, my bad." I was tempted to ask him and the young people he was leading to stop the swearing, but instead directed one of the young ladies in the group to the same man in the front who was still laying laterally on the front seats, passed out cold.

I said, "I am worried about that guy. How about you?". She looked up from her phone, and said without feeling, "Yeah. He's probably dead."

It occurred to me that these kids were rudderless in a way. Does anyone care enough? Do they realize that they matter? Have respect and empathy for others been instilled in these kids? Is it too late to teach them?

Is taking advantage of the bus driver's inability to stop each and every one of the kids to insure they paid their fare a good life skill to practice?

There were many times as a young guy, when I was misguided, and someone took the time to coach me to be a better person. I was lucky that people cared.

I almost wished I could sit them down, get to know them, build trust and attempt to teach them about respect and decency for themselves, each other, and for society, like many of my teacher colleagues do, day after day.

Eventually, our stop came up, and as my wife got off the bus, I looked back at that one young lady, and I noticed that she had returned fixated to her phone. I regretted that I didn't say anything to the group as a whole. I gave the man in the front of the bus a gentle shake. He was breathing and still in nap mode. The bus driver assured me he knew where the man was headed, and that he was in good hands. I wish I could be sure that I knew where these kids were moving in life.

At the time, I was reading a book written by reporter Chris Matthews. It was about John F. Kennedy and his enigmatic personality. I am still inspired by the way our former president from the 60's energized many to want to do more for their country. I continually fall short, but am reminded that you and I have the potential to do great things for our society and at a minimum for our families, friends and those we may not see eye to eye with.

Someone Gave Me a Talking To

For a period of time, I worked with a young man who was bullied as a child, and refused to go to school, because it was just too painful. Even though some parents might think this young man should buck up and face life, I was surprised by how some incident or multiple things in life can truly affect how we view the world.

I also, had a student say "Dr. Kotz - Why are some people so mean?" I was kind of dumbstruck by the question, but when you teach high school, you do see many cases of this kind of awful behavior, and it hurts my heart.

I also see so much good.

Whether it is seeing students unselfishly give to the Christmas basket drive for those who are less fortunate; or I see students take leadership roles in assemblies, where we have poignant talks, or a sing-along, it gives me hope to see that our young folks are very good at heart.

We have to believe in them, and give guidance when needed to help them see for themselves what good behavior is.

I was tipped off about some guys who bragged on Twitter to another school that they could cheat in a few classes easily. When confronting these individuals (all good men), immediately the defenses came up, but upon reflection, they realized

1) it wasn't the right thing to do
2) wasn't smart to brag about it on a somewhat universal social medium
3) Are you really making good decisions for your life?

It made me think back to when I lived in Buffalo, NY as a kid, and was invited to my friend's family picnic. We were flinging a football around, and laughing it up, while the scent of outdoor cooking permeated the air.

A throw by my friend Tim hit me in the chest pretty hard, and I yelled out, "F%$#".

I will never forget how it seemed to me that the entire O'Brien clan looked at the 9 year old me, and one of the older brothers said, "Kid watch your language. We do not like that kind of talk around here, and if you want to be with us and have dinner with us, then you better check that mouth of yours!" I was embarrassed, astonished and ashamed at the same time.

In hindsight over 40 years ago, I am thankful that someone pulled me aside and let me know what was acceptable. As a result of that lesson, and many others, I am still trying to instill that same sense of decorum with our kids today.

Since it has been demonstrated that I am clearly fallible myself, I may not be the best source of delivery of this message.

But, the fact of the matter is that we as adults do try and continue to try to give our young people a sense of what are wise choices to make. Experience is our key to wisdom. Granted, it isn't always appreciated at the time, but like me, it resonates in my mind and heart each time I speak, to be respectful of other people.

We also Need the Young to Inspire Us

Alvin Toffler (a current writer and futurist) asserted that: "The message communicated to most young people today by the society around them is that they are not fully needed, that the society will run itself quite nicely until they - at some distant point in the future - will take over the reigns. Yet this society is not running itself nicely... because the rest of us need all the energy, brains, imagination and talent that young people can bring to bear down on our difficulties."

For society to attempt to solve its desperate problems, (and each generation has them), without the full participation of even very young people is not a good use of the resources we have in this nation.

I believe that our younger generation has so much to offer, and ask that we continue to believe in their innovation and fresh outlook to handle some of the problems of today and tomorrow.

Kindness

Kindness Begets Kindness

I just wanted to get some gas for my car. All I wanted was 87 octane unleaded. The voice from the loudspeaker, since I paid with credit card was "Pump #3, I'm sorry, but only premium and diesel are available." I turned around to see I was the only one at the entire station, gas prices had just gone down to under 2 bucks, and I was perplexed that no one else was around. Then I looked at the pump prices and premium was 10 cents more a gallon. Now, I get why no one was at the pump.

Since I needed a bit more than half a tank, and my daughter had to get to her volunteer opportunity, I just dug my heels in and let the automatic fill up take place with "premium" gas.

As we went into get coffee, the pleasant voice of the cashier remained in my ears. "You have a voice for radio", I said. The lady I faced, said, "That wasn't me, that was her!", and she pointed to another lady behind the registers.

She laughed, and my daughter and I proceeded to get a coffee. The lady at the register said, "Is that your daughter?"

"Yes", I said.

"Your daughter is so pretty." My kid was beaming. Kindness begets kindness, and it's also just fun to make people smile.

Sure enough, I drive 23 miles to take Kali to her volunteer opportunity, only to find that the Walker Elder Suites has a flu outbreak, and Kali isn't expected to work.

You'd think someone would call to let her know. Oh, well back to reality. In this case, thank you for cell phones. At the time, I didn't have one, but Kali did, and here, it came in handy, and she called me at work.

So, a lunch, and discussing this experience with my daughter once again, helped me to see that people just want some recognition, some attention, and some love.

The Power of Encouragement

The power of encouragement is enchanting to me. I attended a capstone presentation for a student soon to graduate, who admitted that he didn't have many people supporting him in life. The week had been eventful already, and I was bushed.

But, a month before and again on Friday evening, he asked me if I could attend. I made a commitment a month ago to see him in his final hour of grad work.

By Friday afternoon, I truly wanted to decline. But, to see this young man shine that evening, beam with competence, and that he had other people to witness his talent, expertise, and new found knowledge - was well worth the trip.

It does make a difference in multi-fold ways, when we support each other. This individual, I believe, will do great things, rippling out his own waves by encouraging others in our society, because he also knows that he too, was once supported to be braver than he believed, stronger than he felt, and given the tools to see that he too, was more talented than he once believed.

Society Today

Are We Moving Too Fast?

A letter from an adult without kids:

"I do not have kids but my sense is they feel that they want now what their parents have worked years to get. Do you think that is the case or am I am overly sensitive?"

My response:

I believe that we have a society that is so used to the immediate gratification "wanting now" (which can be good in terms of productivity), and we as Americans are also so preoccupied with our own busy lives, that our children have become so good at multi-tasking, and not good at pursuing topics and social issues at great depth.

They have greater wealth than any other prior generation, and have access to more than our generation ever had in terms of options. (This may now be debatable).

I do not think we are taking enough time to enjoy or see the value of the discoveries we have created. We want the latest and the greatest.

Will there come a time when we are so saturated with all these new advances, that we will return to just spending time with one another? That being said, I believe many of our youth are very conscious of health issues, and are extremely bright.

The ability to say "thank you" is not as common as I'd like to hear. People rush by each other, and 1 out of 5 say "excuse me", if they get in someone else's way. (Note my statistic is a random sample, and based on my own observations :).

Distracted

There is a disconnect that has occurred in our society, where we all are so wired that we can't stay focused on someone for more than 10 seconds without getting distracted.

Maybe people just aren't worth talking to for more than this?

My heart tells me otherwise, and suggests to me that we are concentrating way too much on diversions, instead of being fully present with our fellow man and woman. Our work life does dictate what we put our hours into, and yet even our time away from the job is spent emailing, checking messages, and responding back to messages.

Even though some of my emails I receive are about Viagra, or enhancing hair growth.

Maybe, in my case I could restore some hair on my head. I'm not sure if I want to get a rug, weave, or I will just deal with male pattern baldness, or shave my head completely. But, I digress.

See I got distracted! Does this happen to you? If you're like most of us, you probably do get preoccupied with another thought much more than you were expecting.

The Perfect Pickle

At the State Fair, I waited in line at "The Perfect Pickle" along with many individuals. I considered why we pay an entrance fee at the gates to wait in line for delicious items, and then pay again for the item. But, this thought was soon disrupted.

An older couple in front of me was graciously allowing scooter carts and others to walk in front of them to head down the block toward other delicious venues.

All of a sudden, a mother and her child tried to cut in line to get some deep fried pickles, and the lady from the patient couple in front of me politely says, "The line is back there." Sure enough, the mother with child, yells "B$t!&".

I am thinking "great message for your child", and how some of us have lost the idea that respect for one another is so important. There are plenty of good people out there, but it can seem less so when events like this occur.

Finding Where You Belong

On the other hand, Jan and I tried to move a table into a U-Haul, and then eventually into the house. Two gentlemen kindly helped us get the table in and out of the truck.

And, then tonight, with the start of evening classes, one young man thought he had the right room, but was in the wrong building. I walked him toward where he needed to go, and he said, "Sir. Thanks."

Finally, a woman was frantically trying to find her classroom. "There is no 3rd floor in this building!" I agreed with her. I discovered that she had interchanged the numbers and that we had another case of being in the wrong building.

She was distraught, so I also brought her to class a few buildings away from Brother Louis Hall to LaSalle Hall, and told her "People confuse these buildings all of the time", that she was not too late, and it will all be alright. As I was walking away, she gave me a big hug from the side and said, "Thank you, so much."

It is not often I get a hug for finding a room.

Women are Beautiful

Women are beautiful. As a man, I feel lucky and blessed that God gave me a counterpart gender that can provide perspective, insight, intelligence, and guidance each day, at home and in the workplace. Also, at times, as a man, I may truly need to hear when I am off course, or am just plain wrong.

I also think women are beautiful because they are leaders, mothers, mentors, nurturers, champions, and teachers. Since, my wife and two daughters make up the heart and soul of my own family, my perspective on issues of equality and harassment have gradually galvanized, as I continue to grow and change with these priceless partners.

The fact remains that many men continue to think they own the place. I still hear that it is a "man's world". Yes, we men have strengths that can complement a woman's abilities such as collaborating, analyzing a situation, balancing several work/life issues at once, and possessing the endurance to keep going when she has little left to give for the day.

All of this may happen while she is suffering from a cold/flu wearing her down, or knowing that she has to pick up the kids from soccer, piano, or debate team – all after a full day of work.

The fact also remains that we men can be very visually oriented, and do see the aesthetic beauty of women, and appreciate it. I consider that a gift.

But, it is a problem when we, as men, exploit this gift, treat women like objects, lesser beings, pay them at 70% to 80% of what men make in business and industry, and do not see that this valuable feminine perspective is invaluable to making our families, schools, and companies a better place to be.

Actions Speak Louder than Words

Back on August 25, 2001 the KKK came to the St. Paul State Capitol to speak about hate, recruit other members, and keep/revitalize their power in this country. If you recall, 17 days later we were all changed by 9/11, and the U.S. united and came together.

Many of us lost loved ones: brothers, sisters, friends, mentors, and fellow Americans, who we somehow bonded with in unity and grief.

I have never forgotten either one of these days, and I was one of those who attended the rally on that hot August day to send the Klan packing, with limited results.

One of the beauties of free speech is that it allows us to voice our views, still be able to stand on our own two feet, continue with daily life, agree or disagree, all while still retaining respect for one another.

When we get to the point where we divide because of a lack of respect for skin color, gender differences, the way a person talks, their beliefs, or because they just do not agree with us, then we defeat the purpose of what it means to have freedom.

Talk is cheap. We have all heard that actions speak louder than words. We also have plenty of areas of concern to fear outside our own borders as a nation, for us to start fearing each other in daily interaction.

We are too good of a people to live in fear. We all have this goodness; we need to look for it, and in my humble opinion, stop seeing what divides us, but look at others' strengths and learn from them, build on them, complement them with our own, and respect our humanity. Our world needs all of us to love and respect one another. To me, there is no other way.

Clearing the Air

We moved into our home back in 1997, and inherited with our purchase an alley that was all grass. It was supposedly inaccessible to all homes adjacent to the alley property, but occasionally someone would haul some things into their yard, and no one seemed to mind. With this alley came the inevitable time to mow it, and since our backyard faced two other homes' backyards, we were supposed to take turns mowing it.

Mind you, it belongs to the city, but the city would only come back if there was a crisis with power lines, or a tree had to be removed due to Dutch elm disease.

For years, I had cut the lawn in the alley along with my neighbor Dorothy. Some would cut half the alley, but since I was the youngest of the bunch, I decided to take the task on with regular fervor.

It also helped me lose some weight. It was a sizeable amount of land, and after you cut your own lawn, would at times feel a little overwhelming. So, my method was to cut our front, and back, usually the same day, and do the alley the next day.

I would load up with gas; and brace myself for the crap that was thrown in the alley. Sometimes, a metal ball bearing, or machine part hidden in the grass blades; or those pesky sticks, which generally fell from one of our trees., would cause the mower blades to sputter.

I was all ready to go, when I noticed a huge bundle of sticks stacked near our fence in the alley. A message was being communicated: "Don't put these on our side of the alley."

I was a little taken aback.

Does it ever irk you that we do not communicate directly with people? Sometimes, we do things in a subtle manner. Nothing is especially wrong with this. I just needed some clarification. And face-to-face was what I needed at this juncture.

So, I walked around the block, and decided to go see the people, who apparently moved the sticks to our side of the alley. A lady with forearms like Popeye answered the door, and I said, "Hi my name is Paul and I live behind you. I cut the lawn behind you and wandered why you moved all of the sticks over to our side of the alley?"

"You cut it!? Dorothy said she always cuts it. We just removed brush back there, and then I see more sticks behind our fence - that is why I moved it!"

"Oh, I see. I can understand why you would be upset. That's why I came over here. I just wanted to let you know I'm not some villain or bad guy throwing sticks on your side. But, in my years of cutting the lawn, I move them to this place, because my blades get stuck, with too much brush."

"Anyway, I thought I would stop by and clear the air."

"Are you done?" she tersely quipped.

"Yes. I am. Have a nice day. And say hello to me when I am back there. I could use some morale support."

As I was walking away, she said, "Is there something you are trying to tell me?"

"Well, I wanted to let you know that our intentions are good. I use my gas money, pick up the brush, insure the alley is not overgrown, and it would be nice in all these years to have a thank you."

"I didn't realize you cut it. Again, Dorothy said she does it."

"I respect Dorothy. She does cut it at times too, and I'm sure she did prior to when we moved in. She did it much of the time."

"Now I know," she said. The lady seemed to have calmed down.

We laughed a little, and then I ambled back to my home, content that I spoke my mind, but not entirely sure, if she thought I was an ass. But, what I did learn is that many times we misunderstand each other, and we could instead maybe make a new friend, if we would just be patient with one another, and not jump to conclusions.

Mentoring

High School Excuses and Happenings

Mr. Kotz – "What do you think of my eyebrow earring? My friend helped me."

"The earring looks great, but your eyebrow is swelling, dear, and looks infected."

Can I go to the bathroom?

Is this going to be a fun day?

Can we color today?

Can this be a chill day?

Why is it always so cold in here?

Why is it always so hot in here?

Can I have a Kleenex?

Just one, not three! I am on a budget.

How was I supposed to know that if 50 of us bounced superballs all at once in the hallways that someone would get hit in the eye?!

Why can't we have short schedules every day?

We have a test today?!

I left my book in my stepdad's girlfriend's car!

You're not going to believe this but the reason my geometry homework is missing, is because our house burned down.

Can I see the nurse?

My colleague had asked kids to provide a picture of a graph with their homework problems, and one kid attached a Polaroid of their graphing calculator. Nice.

Why can't I have this food in the classroom? I am hungry. 3 bags of chips. 2 vitamin waters, and a breakfast burrito.

Really – my mom is trying to call me. It's a medical emergency! (cell phone)

Reflection on the Daily Life of Teaching

I feel like I make an impact teaching and trying to be a role model, and then other times, I feel like I'm the adult, busting a kid for using drugs or substances in school, and then subsequently ruining the kid's life, because he has to be suspended, and must go in for treatment.

At the same time, you have this senior girl who sends you a typed note that borders on a being too personal, saying you're her favorite teacher, because you made her feel special, and pushed her to limits academically she never thought she could achieve.

One moment a kid says you are a great person, and the next moment you are the imposing figure who gave them too much homework, and ruined their social life.

Fulfilling, exhausting, exhilarating...Not a bad life.

A Day in the Life of Teaching High School

Sometimes you hit your limits as a teacher. Kids incessantly talk and then expect you to ensure that they do not fall behind, when they are really in jeopardy of not passing or getting a grade less than their own expectations. At one time, I removed a senior from one of my classes because they were extremely disruptive and were not using their potential.

As a matter of historical record, I have removed young adults temporarily out of my class for a variety of circumstances:

1. Disrespect
2. Incessant talking after repeated warnings
3. Drug or alcohol usage
4. Cheating
5. Harassing others
6. Not using their potential

In some cases, after I have sent the young person out of class, saying, "You do not return, until you write me a letter stating why you should be allowed to return." As a result of the dismissal, I have seen parents act as a defense attorney for their young ones, call the principal, and claim that the teacher is the one who was out of line.

Now, granted, there are times when I feel I could have handled an issue in another manner, such as "Johnny (Sara), you will need to leave my class now. Too many warnings have been given, and now you should go to the dean of students. Take your books and go quietly."

Now, there are a few kids, from my experience, who do not go quietly, and furthermore, are oblivious to the idea that they could have committed such an infraction as disturbing the teacher or another classmate. Also, granted that louder kids seem to catch my attention more than quiet ones, or more surreptitious types, who can pull a prank possibly unnoticed, or slyly that they are seldom caught.

Other times, I have had kids who have been sent to the library/or testing center to take an exam, and then go ahead and cheat in front of a school camera, and continually deny that they would do such a thing, until I pull out my Ace in the hole, and remind them that we have their actions on tape.

Would they like to tell me what really happened? I believe I have a good deal of patience, and truly care about teaching.

It's these other issues, which are at times humorous, but also present a challenge. For instance, I once had a kid hand me a worksheet under the stall of the men's room, and ask me: "Mr. Kotz, I realize this is awkward, but could you help me find X?".

He wasn't even in my class. I said, "I could help you find some manners. But, no X at this time."

"Stop and see me after school. I'll be there if you need help." But this is another story entirely.

It seems that a human defensive nature kicks in when a parent meeting is called, and we want to see our own kids in the best light possible. But, somewhere along the line parents have to give the teacher the benefit of the doubt, and accept that their kid was/could have been out of control, even if for the moment or a class period.

It is possible. Think of the hormones, as an added bonus to the situation.

I wish I could say I was a perfect angel in high school. In my day, if you were talking, a teacher could rap you on the side of the head.

Or because I was conversing during class, instead of paying attention, the teacher drew two circles on the board, and had me put my index fingers in them, while taking a step backward, remaining standing, until the instructor, in this case gave you the word that you can remove your hands from the board.

After 45 seconds, a serious pain develops in one's hand. Nonetheless, I stopped talking, when the teacher was conducting class.

If I did this to a young person today, much less kick a student out (remove them from the situation), I would possibly lose my position, or be sued for hurting the child's self esteem.

So in my case, (after the call on cell phone, and the retreat to the counselor had already taken place) I went to see my principal, who luckily respected my way of dealing with kids, because I seldom if ever have to resort to such measures as telling a kid to "Shut Up! I have asked you many times, and it doesn't seem to change. Leave. And go to Mr. M".

Nowadays, kids in trouble do not always go where they are supposed to go. Some will make calls to their parents complaining of their harsh treatment. Some will even tape the teacher with a hidden cell phone/camera to make them look foolish, and some will go to a more friendly audience, such as a counselor - Instead of going to see the person who you intended them to see!

My principal once sighed and said, "I understand where you are coming from, and your frustration." She had a few parent meetings for similar incidences, and said that it is hard as a teacher much less a human being to let go of an episode so soon after it has happened.

I for one, question how I could have done it differently, or whether I was too harsh. Was I too lenient? Should I have just looked the other way, and let the kid do exactly what they want or perceive as appropriate behavior?

There was a moment of silence. My principal lapsed into a story, which made me smile. Her dream involved being very sick, and being too ill to get out of bed, even though she had five parent meetings that day.

But somehow, she ended up coming to school for all 5-parent meetings. Her bed was wheeled into her executive office, and she heard parent defenses and complaints systematically for much of the day, all the while being sick with flu preceded by heavy temperature and nausea.

This was only a dream, but it manifests the stress that many people in the teaching environment go through in their quest to mold and shape our young children.

The Cerebral Cortex is Not Fully Developed

Some parents have said that it is our job as teachers to teach the subject, and it is the parent's job to worry about how their kid should be acting. I agree, but the teacher takes on this added responsibility daily, as less and less parents trust the judgments of the teacher, and rely on their own young people, whose cerebral cortex is still in a maturation process, and is not always apt to be so forthcoming right away, and not always the most rational.

What Students Expect

I have found that no matter the level you teach at, students want you as an instructor/facilitator to be responsive to their ever-changing needs, and yet set the bar high for them to be challenged and meet their goals.

I have worked as an on-ground instructor in undergraduate research courses, ethics, and statistics and have been a dissertation mentor for doctoral programs for a number of years.

Here I have found our diverse student body to be balancing so many different aspects of their lives: work, family, meeting deadlines for assignments, and allowing time for themselves can be quite a juggling match.

"Being fair with students, and setting reasonable expectations, and providing a friendly tone in interactions" are what students have given me as advice over the years.

I have synthesized this down to being "Fair, firm, and friendly" with each student or person I encounter. Some schools are truly providing the flexibility to meet career goals and still meet family and personal needs. I have grown to appreciate that all of us are trying to balance so many aspects of our lives.

Unexpected Surprises

Half of the Moon is Visible

On a Saturday, the dawn sun had just come up. I stepped into the backyard to feel the crisp, cool air of Autumn. My daughter was also up early, and I asked her to check out the heavens with me. We both looked up into the sky, and I pointed out to her that we had a "Half Moon" visible.

I said to her that it reminds me of the notion that "even though we only see half the moon this morning, there is still a full moon - half we can see, and half that is hidden.

"That hidden part is a lot like our own hidden potential." My daughter smiled, and I am not entirely sure what she thought at that moment.

But, it made me realize......Even though our entire self is not visible to the people we encounter daily, we have much that is latently hidden, untapped, or not fully substantiated. We have the capability to unleash this latent self in an undeniably positive way.

It is Mysterious How God Works

It is a mysterious way in how God works. I have a good friend from Kenya, who stayed with us, and who enjoyed his first time in the U.S. He has a wonderful family back home and had a short term action-packed, one-week stay with us.

One day my wife and I had planned an evening dinner for my international friend, only to find earlier in the day, that his father had died. Being thousands of miles from home, and realizing that he wanted to be there for his immediate family and father had to be very difficult and painful. His dad had been ill before he had departed, but told him to go. "It is an incredible opportunity. Do it."

So I had to handle a few work issues on this unsettling day, and on my way to campus, was listening to a melancholy but lovely song called "Rainy Day Feeling Again" by the Fortunes. I had to try to keep it together, but on the way to work that afternoon, cried thinking of my friend's predicament and feeling what he was going through.

Many of us have lost loved ones, and you know what I am saying.

It is out of your control. But, I realized that what was not out of our control as a community was doing our best to have a memorable Kenyan party sendoff for our friend.

Luckily I have friends, family, and colleagues who came to make his night brighter, just laugh, and tell stories. No mention was made at the party of the loss of his father, but a few of us knew and felt his dad's presence.

Sometimes you just move forward. It is guaranteed that you will step back into your grief and loss, feel the pain, the joy, and those places where you are not sure what your next step should be.

But, somehow, you are here today for a reason. God gave you life and the gift of "you".

Snow on the Back of the Windshield

On a wintery morning on my way to work, I noticed a St. Paul police car waiting at the stop light in front of me, with snow completely covering the back of the windshield.

I thought to myself…should I take my brush and clear it off for this one squad car of many, whose officers protect us each day?

A few things raced through my mind quickly, such as "What if the police misinterprets this, and thinks I am interfering with public property?" or "Maybe, they'll think I am trying to vandalize his/her back window?" I realize that some of you will think I am a few fries short of a happy meal.

It was a red light, and I decided to get out of my car, and do it anyway. The officer popped his head out of the window, kind of astonished, and I said: "Thanks for all you do. Have a good day!"

He drove off, without a word. I discussed this with a colleague of mine, who said, "I could never do that, as a black person, in our society." He also commented, "That was very brave. For me, it would be insane."

It made me think that if we can't do something positive, without the constant judgment being made of our intentions, actions or color of our skin, that we may need to once again reconsider if we truly are living in a free, just and trusting society.

St. Anthony and an Unexpected Coincidence

On January 12th, 2007, Jan and I took my mom, Rita out to Carbone's with the girls. Rita tells us about her St. Anthony statue and how the clover started growing out of his hands (The statue is made of stone).

She pulls out a picture she took of the event. I'm giving her some crap, saying she probably glued it on to his palm, so we all thought it was a miracle. How cynical of me, but you can't be too sure these days.

Lo and behold, we are at the St. Paul Carbone's, and in walks the lady who my mom gave the statue to when she moved out of the West St. Paul neighborhood to her condo.

Now, if that isn't divine? She comes up from behind my mom, and touches her shoulders.

"Marlene!" I exclaim. We were just talking about you. Her husband says, "It can't all be good!" I replied, "This is!".

The odds of that happening are pretty slim, but I think God was listening. My mom and Marlene chatted as if nothing monumental had happened, but I thought that was a spiritually guided moment, which I cannot fully explain, but I was kind of in awe, with my mouth agape.

Jan said incredulously, "Is that the lady who Rita gave the statue to?"

I said, "Yes it is". We both stared at each other dumbfounded.

Maybe it was just a coincidence, but I still think some higher power was guiding this chance meeting.

You are in for a Delightful Surprise

We have hurricanes, which devastate regions. Typhoons loom in the gulf to wreak havoc. And, somewhere a dictator is making escalating threats for the world to contend with. Meanwhile, on a day after Labor Day, I share another small life vignette.

I grabbed some lunch at a Chinese takeout restaurant, and asked the man at the counter how he was doing and how his weekend was.

He said, "Ok. I worked yesterday, and it was constantly busy. Doesn't anyone want to barbecue outside anymore?!" This guy looked like he could use a break.

Meanwhile, it looked like the boss in the back was barking out commands to ensure they had enough supplies and food for the week of service to customers at Lee Ann Chin.

I opened my fortune cookie where it read: "You are in for a delightful surprise." I looked up, and saw the man, again who served me, emptying the trash and moving at a quick pace.

I took out a gift card from my wallet for Pazzaluna. I like this place, but thought it would be good to give it to the man who was working hard on Labor Day. He approached my table, and asked how everything was, and I said it was wonderful. I was starved, and it hit the spot.

I said, "Here. This is for you. Take a date out to this restaurant, and have a great time." I also gave him my fortune message, but made sure to eat the cookie.

He looked a bit shocked, and said, "Thanks, man." He was definitely smiling, and actually had a spring in his step, when he cleared off the next table.

I said, "Let me know how it goes." And, then I left to face the rest of what more of life's mysteries are in store.

Advice and Perspectives

An Uninteresting life?

"An uninteresting life? That is impossible. Even the person with the dullest of exteriors, has an inner life of some drama, a bit of comedy, and some tragedy." Mark Twain

Fair, Firm and Friendly

I have observed that if you are fair, firm and friendly, (in general) you will be listened to more often than not.

One of the Greatest Gifts

I have found that one of the greatest gifts in life is to connect with the heart and soul of at least one other person.

Hold On with Both Hands

If you haven't figured it out by now...not everyone is going to like you. And for those people that do see the good in you, treasure it, and hold on with both hands.

People Leave Footprints

"You will never know true happiness until you have truly loved, and you will never understand what pain really is until you have lost it. Some people come into our lives, leave footprints in our hearts, and we are never ever the same." But, it is definitely worth the sacrifice.

The Best Kinds of People

Something to ponder: The best kinds of people are the ones that come into your life, and make you see the sun and stars where you once saw clouds and darkness. The people that believe in you so much, you start to believe in you too. The people that love you, simply for being you. The once in a lifetime kind of people.

Love isn't Easy

"Love isn't easy. Especially the really good kind. It's difficult, and you'll want to rip your hair out just as many days as you'll feel the

73

wind at your back. But it's worth it. It's worth fighting for. Don't let what isn't real blind you from what is. Life isn't perfect, we sure as shit aren't perfect, so why should we expect love to be?" Nicole Williams

You Can't Make Someone Love You

"I've learned that you cannot make someone love you. All you can do is be someone who can be loved. The rest is up to them."

Making Mistakes is Okay

Those who do not make mistakes, do not make anything.

Cleaning Your Own Room

A wise person once said to me: "Sometimes you may not have to change your entire life. At this point, you may have to just clean your own room."

Gratitude and Eating

Sometimes a little gratitude for the gifts you have been given and acceptance can help carry you through difficult times. Also, a Juicy Lucy and/or a Nut Goodie can help.

Pick Others Up

"Never look down on anybody unless you're helping them up." Reverend Jesse Jackson

If You are Kind

"If you are kind, people may accuse you of selfish motives. Be kind anyway.

If you are honest and sincere, people may deceive you. Be honest anyway.

People are often unreasonable and self-centered. Forgive them anyway.

The good you do today will often be forgotten. Do good anyway." Unknown

Give Your Best

"Give the best you have and it will never be enough. Give your best anyway."

"In the final analysis, it is between you and God. It was never between you and them anyway." - Mother Teresa

Kindness is Never Wasted

"No act of kindness, however small, is ever wasted." Aesop (I hung this in my classroom for years)

More Life Advice

When you find yourself in a rut, do something new to get out of it!

"It's kind of fun to do the impossible." --Walt Disney

You can go through life thinking nothing is a miracle, (or as I believe along with Einstein), that everything is a miracle, and happens for a reason.

"Don't worry about being everything to everyone, but try to be something to someone."

When you make the biggest mistake ever, something good will even come from that.

Live a Good and Honorable Life

Someone once told me: "Live a good and honorable life. That way, when you look back on it you can enjoy it a second time."

Pretend Like it's 1995

I was thinking about the recent story of the guy who went on a date (he had met online) and asked for his $17.31 back. His story was that his date texted as soon as she arrived in the theater to meet him, and he asked if she could put her cell away for a while.

She then walked out. He was miffed by this and soon after asked for his money back. She claimed, "It was just a date."

It occurred to me that we may eventually communicate by exclusively texting, with less face-to-face interaction. Also, some say it is much easier to text someone than to talk to them directly.

It also made me think that newer generations may one-day cycle back to the idea of having less technology driven interactions, and more face-to-face dialogue.

Some young people have told me that they start to feel anguish if they do not have enough "likes" on their Facebook posts, and if they do not meet a certain standard such as 100, then they have failed.

Possibly, civility standards or decorum in communication could be instilled in kids at earlier ages, since this is the world we/they live in. I realized that once you have a cell phone, it is an integral part of your life, and possibly an extra appendage to your hand.

In a bar, I saw a sign that craved the past: "No cell phones allowed. Pretend like it is 1995, and talk to someone."

Problems Created by Hate

I have seen many problems created by hate, and rarely one solved by it.

Stars and Sun

You cannot see the stars in the daytime. But they are still there. You also cannot see the sun when it is night. But, again, it is still there.

The Last Lecture

I read the book *A Team of Rivals* about the Civil War, and the diplomatic sagacity of Abraham Lincoln. As Stanton, his Secretary of War, remarked at Lincoln's death: "He is now one for the ages." He is a president who had such an impact on our future, our present, and how we interact with each other.

"United we stand, divided we fall" are words that I truly think are relevant for today's world. How often do we compete with someone? Whether it's our friends, family, or ourselves? Do we try to work together?

So often, it's about being right, versus, how can we see the other person's side? Sometimes, we care too much with good intentions, meddling with other's lives, when we may not know the whole story.

Often, I wonder, how could I have handled a difficult situation differently? Lincoln could have brought an iron fist down on the surrendering South in the Civil War, but instead, let the prisoners go free, assisted slaves in acquiring freedom (even though initially he was hesitant), and made the provision to all citizens that they have to promise not to try to break the country apart again.

This takes wisdom, but also the ability to listen. When you win, often you want to squelch your opponent with no mercy. Lincoln saw beyond that, and had a broader vision for our nation, which desperately needed to heal. Unfortunately, after so much trial and loss of life, he was slain by an assassin's bullet, only to have his miraculous deeds be resurrected by countless books, and remembrances.

I was also struck by thoughts from *The Last Lecture*, which sprang forth from an individual dying from pancreatic cancer.

Do we truly say we are sorry? How can I make it right?

Machiavelli would say this makes one weak to apologize: "It is better to be feared, than loved." There might be some merit to this, if we want to have more division than unity in our world.

I have grown to believe that I would rather err on the side of kindness than being the strongest. Maybe strength through kindness is truly possible.

Waiting for Good Pitches

My daughter, Becca asked me to help her with her softball hitting in the summer of 2007. She wanted to be ready for her game the next day, and wanted to practice.

I remember telling my daughter three things during softball batting practice, because I thought they made sense when someone told me.

"Remember to watch the ball."

"Secondly, know where your sweet spot in the strike zone is, and don't swing at every first pitch. Make sure it's a good pitch."

The latter one came back to haunt me. We go to the park, and I bring 12 balls from previous coaching experiences, and pitch to my daughter.

There are few kids available to catch, so the ball hits the backstop, or she hits them in the outfield, and then we go get the balls, and start anew.

It was kind of fun, but in the sweltering heat in July, it can get kind of labor intensive. Anyway, I said to Becca, since this is just practice, if the pitches are close you can go for them.

She said to me, "I don't swing at the first pitch anymore. I wait for good pitches."

You Don't Know What it Means to Be Me

I think of the daily news and how much it centers on information leaks, political positioning, whether we will have liquor sales on Sunday, whether a politician swayed the election or not, or even the latest box score for a sporting event. This is life, and each of us goes in directions that bring us some joy, satisfaction, or to something that sparks our interest. But, when a crisis develops for someone we know or one of us slips up, we often rush to judgment.

In essence, we don't know what it means to be that person. That is, I am not sure that we truly know what it means to walk in their shoes.

I saw the fabulous Norah Jones, and in her concert she temporarily moved away from soulful and sultry to rocking out on an electric guitar singing, "You don't know what it means to be me." It made me reflect. We never truly know the plight people are going through, unless we ask.

What Brings You Happiness?

Are you really happy? It's a question that has crossed all of our minds. Just a month prior to reading about the researcher, explorer and best-selling author Dan Buettner, I had been wrestling with this question myself.

"Am I really happy?"

I know I am passionate about the work that I do. And, I love my family and friends.

My faith is at the core of my being. And I really appreciate the little things in life: the sunshine in my face while walking around a lake, a rainy Monday, the color of fall (one of my favorite times of the year), my morning drive listening to the news, that special song that sparks a memory, and the laughter of children and adults.

For me it's these little things that seem to make me happy. But is that really enough?

I learned a considerable amount from Buettner, who traveled the world in search of the keys to happiness. His National Geographic book, "Thrive: Finding Happiness the Blue Zones Way," revealed secrets from the world's happiest people.

Based on his research, these fortunate people reside in Mexico, Denmark, Singapore, and San Luis Obispo, California. And, since the majority of us do not live in those places, he came up with the "special sauce" to happiness that we can add to our lives so that we, too, can thrive.

According to Buettner, there are six areas that we should focus on that lead to ultimate happiness: 1. home, 2. self, 3. financial life, 4. social life, 5. workplace, and 6. community.

Each area contributes to our overall well-being or lack thereof. Where you live, volunteering your time, connection in a faith-based community, socializing regularly, picking a fulfilling job, and choosing the right mate are all important factors in finding happiness, no matter where you live.

Maybe, spending money on more experiences and less things. Maybe, a talk with a good friend about a recent book we both read; or playing a sport with other competitors who enjoy it to the same degree.

Trying to sing, even though not everybody wants you to; travelling, volunteering or teaching others a new skill – some might take up tae kwon do lessons, a knit-and-crochet workshop, or book a two-week-long African safari.

When You Figure it All Out

And what are you going to do to live a happier life?
When you figure it all out, let me know your secret.

90-Year-Old Advice with
Some Additions from Other Wise Folks

Mostly compiled by those wiser than me and Regina Brett, 90 years old at the time, of Cleveland, Ohio.

1. Life isn't fair, but it's still good.
2. When in doubt, just take the next small step.
3. Life is too short to waste time hating anyone.
4. Your job won't take care of you when you are sick. Your friends and parents will. Stay in touch.
5. Pay off your credit cards every month.
6. You don't have to win every argument. Agree to disagree.
7. Cry with someone. It's more healing than crying alone.
8. It's OK to get angry with God. God can take it.
9. Save for retirement starting with your first paycheck.
10. When it comes to chocolate, resistance is futile.
11. Make peace with your past so it won't screw up the present.
12. It's OK to let your children see you cry.
13. Don't compare your life to others. You have no idea what their journey is all about.
14. If a relationship has to be a secret, you shouldn't be in it.
15. Everything can change in the blink of an eye. But don't worry; God never blinks.
16. Take a deep breath. It calms the mind.
17. Get rid of anything that isn't useful, beautiful or joyful.
18. Whatever doesn't kill you really does make you stronger.
19. It's never too late to have a happy childhood. But the second one is up to you and no one else.
20. When it comes to going after what you love in life, don't take no for an answer.

21. Over prepare. Then go with the flow.
22. Be eccentric now. Don't wait for old age to wear purple.
23. The most important organs you have are your brain and your heart.
24. No one is in charge of your happiness but you.
25. Frame every so-called disaster with these words: 'In five years, will this matter?'
26. Always choose life.
27. Forgive everyone everything.
28. What other people think of you is none of your business.
29. Time heals almost everything. Give time time.
30. Not everyone is going to like you.
31. However good or bad a situation is, it will change.
32. Don't take yourself so seriously. No one else does.
33. Believe in miracles.
34. God loves you because of who God is, not because of anything you did or didn't do.
35. Don't audit life. Show up and make the most of it now.
36. Growing old beats the alternative -- dying young.
37. Your children get only one childhood.
38. All that truly matters in the end is that you loved.
39. Get outside every day. Miracles are waiting everywhere.
40. If we all threw our problems in a pile and saw everyone else's, we'd grab ours back.
41. Envy is a waste of time. You already have all you need.
42. The best is yet to come...
43. No matter how you feel, get up, dress up and show up.
44. Yield.
45. Life isn't tied with a bow, but it's still a gift."

I cannot disagree with any of these.